Lucid Dreaming

Strategies For Harnessing The Potential Of Lucid
Dreaming And Materializing Goals Via The Application Of
Mindfulness And Verification Of Reality

(Methods For Inducing And Regulating Lucid Dreaming)

Gabriel Cartwright

TABLE OF CONTENT

What Is Lucid Dreaming 1

Physical Manifestation: Interplay Between Sex And Astral Projection 40

Experiences Of Astral Projection 49

Mastering Lucid Dreams 93

Instructions For Attaining 103

Strategies For Maintaining Lucidity In Your Dream State 119

Can The Practice Of Lucid Dreaming Facilitate Personal Transformation? 125

Managing And Addressing Sleep Disorders .. 132

What Is Lucid Dreaming

A lucid dream is a profoundly vivid dream in which an individual possesses consciousness of their dreaming state. In the phenomenon of lucid dreaming, individuals typically maintain consciousness within their dream state. Individuals possess the capacity to exercise complete or partial jurisdiction over themselves and their immediate environment.

The level of consciousness that individuals typically possess when they encounter lucidity ranges from a subtle to a highly distinct viewpoint. In the event that an individual becomes aware that they are dreaming while immersed in a typical dream state, this phenomenon is commonly known as a dream-induced lucid dream. A wake-initiated lucid dream refers to the occurrence when an individual seamlessly transitions from a normal waking state into a dream state, without experiencing any gaps in consciousness.

The phenomenon known as lucid dreaming entails the capability of an individual to deliberately guide and manipulate the content of their dreams. It effectively transmutes one's imagined realm into a tangible existence wherein every aspect mirrors real-life authenticity. During a state of clarity, individuals typically become aware of their dream state and their cognitive abilities within the dream will transition towards wakefulness.

It is possible for any individual to acquire the skill of lucid dreaming as it stems from the fact that we all possess the innate ability to experience dreams and subsequently achieve conscious awareness within them. One advantageous aspect of lucid dreaming lies in the capability to exercise control over the content of one's dreams. With this method, you have the opportunity to redefine your aspirations and consequently thrive in exceptional dream encounters. The scope of potential in your dream can be constrained solely by the limitations imposed by your imagination. The phenomenon of lucid dreaming affords individuals the opportunity to explore and manipulate the latent extraordinary capabilities residing within the untapped regions of our cerebral cortex. The phenomenon of lucid dreaming, peculiar though it may appear, is a rigorously researched and acknowledged manifestation of the dream state within the scientific community.

A lucid dream can be substantiated when it meets specific criteria. "The individual must possess an awareness of the following:".

• Their identity.

- The dream environment.
- Significance of the dream.
- Concentration and focus.
- Dream state.
- Memory function.
- Aptitude for decision-making. • Ability to judiciously determine courses of action. • Competence in making informed choices and judgments.

Characteristics of Lucid Dreamers

Not every individual possesses the ability to effectively engage in lucid dreaming. Notwithstanding, there are occasions when individuals undergo lucid dreams. Lucid dreaming is the practice of achieving conscious awareness during one's dreams, and it is a phenomenon that occurs naturally for every individual at least once during their lifetime. It is an aptitude that can be acquired by individuals of all backgrounds and abilities.

(a.) Light sleepers

In order to maintain command over one's dreams, individuals must possess the quality of being easily roused from sleep, as their natural inclination is towards consciousness of self. Individuals who possess a propensity for deep sleep often experience a level of detachment from their surroundings, rendering them essentially in a state of unconsciousness. These individuals remain unruffled even in the face of disruptions.

(b.) Good dream recall

Individuals who possess the ability to experience lucid dreams exhibit impeccable capacity for recollection of their dream content. Individuals who possess a heightened sensitivity to disturbances during sleep tend to experience frequent periods of waking, thereby resulting in an increased capacity to recall dreams. If an individual lacks the ability to recall dreams, the likelihood of achieving lucidity is nearly negligible.

(c.) Good at multitasking

Multitasking entails efficiently managing multiple tasks simultaneously. Lucidity refers to the state of being cognizant that one is immersed in a dream and actively engaging with it. Hence, proficient lucid dreamers are often regarded as adept at multitasking. This necessitates the capacity to exercise control over both the conscious realm of one's mind and the subconscious realm of dreams.

(d.) Creativity

Numerous individuals who experience lucid dreaming showcase a high level of creativity. They possess a remarkable capacity to perceive and cogitate beyond conventional boundaries. Their imaginative faculties can be harnessed and expanded to transcend the boundaries of reality. This attribute affords them the capability to engage in lucid dreaming.

(e.) Risk-takers

During the state of lucid dreaming, individuals encounter events that may induce anxiety, yet adept lucid dreamers adeptly manage such circumstances. Consequently, they are recognized as individuals who are inclined to take risks, as they possess the means to confront their fears by means of lucid dreaming.

Chapter 4: Strategies for Attaining Lucid Dream States

A lucid dream may be induced through various methods. A Dream-Initiated Lucid Dream, commonly referred to as DILD, is initiated with the dreamer experiencing a normal dream, leading to the subsequent realization that it is, in fact, a dream. Conversely, a WILD or Wake-Initiated Lucid Dream occurs when an individual seamlessly transitions from a typical waking state to a dream state, devoid of any discernible interruption in consciousness. Furthermore, the phenomenon known as Wake Induced Lucid Dreaming (WILD) occurs when the dreamer seamlessly transitions into a state of REM sleep while maintaining uninterrupted consciousness, directly from the waking state.

If one desires to undergo the phenomenon of experiencing a lucid dream, there exists a multitude of suggested methodologies. The ability to remember one's dreams is crucial in achieving lucidity during the dreaming state. It is possible that you are acquainted with an individual who maintains a dream journal. Upon awakening from a dream, it is advisable to meticulously document any recollections, irrespective of the occurrence transpiring during nocturnal hours. The underlying tenet is that through consistent focus on your dreams on a daily basis, you will cultivate the inclination to recollect them and discern discernible patterns in the manner in which you dream. Once you have fully acclimated to the intricacies of your dreaming process, you will swiftly refine your aptitude to earnestly observe your own dreamscapes.

Listed below are several approaches to facilitate the experience of lucid dreaming:

Napping

One potential method that could facilitate the occurrence of lucid dreams entails the incorporation of scheduled periods of rest and recuperation. In this approach, it will be necessary to rise at an earlier hour than usual and remain awake for approximately 30 minutes before returning to sleep. Sleep disruption seems to blur the distinction between wakefulness and sleep.

The practice of inducing lucid dreaming through mnemonic techniques (MILD)

This represents one of the proposed strategies put forth by LaBerge. Upon awakening from a dream, it is imperative to make a concerted effort to fully recollect its entirety. While resuming your slumber, maintain a mindful affirmation that you will successfully recollect the state of being in a dream during your subsequent slumber cycle. The subsequent step entails envisioning oneself transported back to the dream experienced a moment ago, and diligently scrutinizing for any discernible sign indicating that the dream is veritably a figment of the imagination rather than actuality.

LaBerge refers to these indications as "dream signs." At this juncture, reiterate to yourself that you are in a dreaming state and sustain the flow of your imagination. Continue executing these actions until you attain a state of slumber.

Reality Testing

This method pertaining to the achievement of lucid dreaming entails maintaining a constant focus on one's conscious state throughout the entirety of the day. This methodology also exhibits connections to the Buddhist concept of mindfulness. The continuous recognition of the current condition you find yourself in is thought to facilitate the exploration of the opposite end of the spectrum. This will facilitate a deeper exploration of consciousness, enabling enhanced recognition of the dream state. In light of everything, how can one ascertain their true state of consciousness? Your actions elicit a logical response. In the realm of dreams, the aforementioned behaviors appear to deviate from a coherent and rational sequence.

The Diamond Meditation Technique

This alternative technique offers a means to cultivate a broader awareness of dreams, thus circumventing the customary steep learning curve associated with attaining lucidity during dreaming. This particular approach can be carried out via the practice of meditation. While engaging in the practice of meditation, endeavor to envision your existence, encompassing both fantastical and factual aspects, as facets of a precious gemstone, namely a diamond. There are individuals who make use of the term "Universe" to designate this "diamond," whereas others utilize the terms "Spirit" or even "God" to describe it. The primary concept is to begin acknowledging that life is occurring simultaneously. Our perspectives alone dictate how we arrange ourselves in a structured manner. Therefore, the experiences of the actual self and the "dreaming self" are indeed shared. This process was also identified and acknowledged by remote viewers. Please be advised that this training necessitates a modest adjustment in one's level of awareness.

Devices and instruments for enhancing lucid dreaming - since the surge in public fascination with lucid dreaming during the 1980s, there has been a growing endeavor to develop the ultimate gadget for facilitating lucid dreams. The aim is to simplify the process of lucid dreaming, enabling individuals to effortlessly engage in it at their discretion.

The prevalent form of lucid dreaming device is an ocular covering capable of transmitting auditory and visual stimuli to the aspiring lucid dreamer during the state of sleep. Usually, this implies that the lucid dreamer would see flashing lights in dreams, which will remind him that he's dreaming. There exist certain options that also offer auditory stimuli.

Here is a selection of the finest lucid dream devices presently accessible within the market. Kindly be advised that lucid dream masks with light-emitting features are not recommended for individuals with photosensitive epilepsy.

Lucid Dream Masks

Utilizing lucid dream masks could potentially facilitate the achievement of your goal to become proficient in lucid dreaming. These masks provide an artificial assistance to enhance your efforts in remembering dreams and assessing reality. Nevertheless, it is important to be aware that there is no absolute assurance that any lucid dreaming device will effectively induce a lucid dream. Furthermore, it should be noted that lucid dream machines do not possess the capacity to enhance one's proficiency in the realm of lucid dreaming. Do not hastily procure lucid dream machines unless you possess a comprehensive understanding of their efficacy in producing desired outcomes. Presented below are several of the most sought-after lucid dream masks currently accessible in the marketplace:

The NovaDreamer, a groundbreaking creation pioneered by the renowned Lucidity Institute. It seems to resemble a fusion of goggles and a sleep mask. The intended purpose of the NovaDreamer is to assist individuals in achieving lucid dreaming by providing alerts when they have entered the rapid eye movement (REM) stage of sleep. The sensors embedded within this device are capable of monitoring ocular movements and subsequently activating an illuminating light directed towards the eyes. Upon viewing the illumination in your dream, you shall come to discern that you are presently immersed in the realm of dreaming.

The REM Dreamer serves as Europe's counterpart to the NovaDreamer, developed by the prestigious Lucidity Institute. The REM Dreamer possesses a multitude of technological attributes and carries a notably lower price compared to the NovaDreamer.

The Remee gained considerable acclaim in 2012 as a cutting-edge sleep mask for facilitating lucid dreaming.

Brainwave and Hypnosis Entrainment

These encompass audio devices that are established upon sound technologies that have been scientifically validated, purporting to aid individuals in attaining a heightened level of meditation and cognitive tranquility. There exists a solid correlation between the practice of frequent meditation and the occurrence of lucid dreaming. Therefore, the act of investing in an appropriate auditory recording that stimulates dreams can also yield remarkable benefits for both the mind and body through meditation. Here are several instances of these audio devices that are currently accessible for commercial purposes.

Lucid dreaming MP3s encompass brainwave entrainment techniques tailored for inducing lucid dreams through both WILD and DILD methods, while also serving as aids for nocturnal meditation.

Lucid Dreaming Hypnosis MP3s – encompassing personalized recordings designed to condition the mind for achieving lucidity through hypnotic autosuggestion. This methodology employs traditional dream imagery.

CDs for Auditory Stimulation – a case in point being Bradley Thompson's Lucid Dreaming Kit, incorporating a CD containing a 72-minute audio simulation and binaural beats.

Sleep Masks

The vast majority of individuals adept at attaining lucidity in their dreams would concur that the preeminent assistive tool to maintain in one's sleeping quarters is a sleep mask. Sleep masks do not only help you retune your Circadian rhythms; they can also help to enhance dream recollection. Sleep masks can facilitate the creation of a sensory-deprived setting conducive to focusing on one's consciousness during WILDS and meditation. The following are the prevailing rationales underlying the usage of sleep masks for the purpose of inducing lucid dreaming:

To engage in the act of meditating during the period of daylight

To foster clarity through simulated awakenings.

To boost dream recall

To balance circadian rhythms

Please find outlined below a selection of superior lucid dreaming sleep masks that are currently procurable on the market:

DreamTime eye pillow for attaining inner peace.

The "Glo to Sleep Eye Mask"

Dream Essentials Sleep Mask with a Contoured Design

Mindfold Sleep and Relaxation Eye Mask offers a tranquil and rejuvenating experience for users.

Dream Essentials Sleep Mask of Exquisite Quality.

Sound Therapy

These machinery options are well-suited for individuals who experience difficulty unwinding at night or face challenges related to excessive mental activity. Here are several prevalent varieties of sound therapy devices currently available in the market:

The Sound Oasis is a sophisticated sound therapy device that incorporates a comprehensive selection of pre-programmed relaxation sound effects and meditative music, facilitating the attainment of profound sleep.

The Sleepsonic is an advanced pillow designed for the purpose of listening to lucid dreaming audios, guided meditation, and brainwave entrainment during the hypnogogic and hypnopompic stages.

Tranquil Turtle, manufactured by Cloud 9, is a calming device that reproduces the sound and ambiance of the ocean. This product was honored with the prestigious Toddler/Infant Toy of the Year Award in 2013.

Certainly, I must emphasize that the acquisition of such devices is not truly essential in order to induce a state of lucid dreaming. If you possess a resilient intellect and possess a heightened state of consciousness, it is highly probable that you would be capable of experiencing the marvels of lucid dreaming by implementing any of the methodologies elucidated within this chapter.

Self-awareness: The cultivation of consciousness

In order to cultivate self-awareness, it is advisable to adhere to the purpose behind the strategies and suggestions, as they serve to facilitate the attainment of one's objectives by enhancing the ease and efficacy of one's actions. We have previously indicated that astral projection may not come easily to every individual.

Now is the opportune moment to embark upon employing these strategies and techniques, which shall assist in facilitating your endeavor towards accomplishing astral travel.

1. Take care of your well-being by paying close attention to your dietary habits, as they directly impact your overall health and vitality. Consuming a plant-based or uncooked nourishment regimen will contribute to an elevation of your vibrational state, leading to a betterment in both your emotional disposition and general well-being. This will enhance the probability of achieving success in future endeavors.

2. Remain relaxed. Retain a state of utmost serenity as you endeavor to attain astral projection. Prior to attempting to dissociate your soul from your physical form, it is advisable to engage in relaxation exercises and employ breathing techniques that facilitate the induction of a hypnotic state. This mental state is essential for successfully accomplishing the task of astral projection.

3. Use sounds. Finding it difficult to unwind amidst utter silence, incorporating sounds like binaural beats can assist in achieving a state of

relaxation. The auditory stimuli will induce a modulation of your cerebral oscillations, consequently facilitating an enhanced state conducive to the attainment of astral projection.

4. Try different methods. There exists no singular method by which you can attain the desired out of body experience. Employ various methodologies and discover the most effective one that suits your needs. There exist methodologies, including the Rope technique and displaced awareness technique, for the purpose of attaining astral travel.

5. Conduct trials with varying periods during the day. The timing and mode of transportation are inconsequential; they are, in fact, subject to individual preferences. Attempt to enter a hypnotic state at various intervals throughout the day in order to ascertain the extent to which your objective can be accomplished. Certain individuals may perceive traveling as more convenient upon awakening, prior to achieving complete awareness of their

surroundings, while others may find it more convenient to engage in travel just before retiring to bed, as a means to alleviate the pressures experienced throughout the day.

6. Release fear. Astral projection may incite fear or apprehension. The sensations experienced by your body are entirely typical to induce fear. The crucial aspect is to refrain from harboring fear towards them; instead, endeavor to wholeheartedly accept them. Any form of diversion, such as the emotion of fear, will disrupt your state of deep concentration and impede your ability to return to the heightened mental state that you diligently cultivated.

7. Be patient. Merely because initial attempts at astral projection do not yield success does not imply permanent incapacity to accomplish it. Continue to practice until you acquire increased confidence and proficiency to achieve the desired outcome.

8. Want to project. It is imperative that there is alignment between your mental and physical state, with both being inclined towards the desire to engage in travel. A mere sense of curiosity would prove insufficient to facilitate travel. It is imperative to possess a resolute determination and earnest longing to separate oneself from the physical vessel.

9. Learn more. Research has proven to be innocuous to individuals, and conversely, the acquisition of knowledge leads to better outcomes.

10. Step back from your immediate vicinity. Upon the moment when you have vacated your physical form, distance yourself from it. The physical bond that binds your soul to your corporeal form possesses the ability to swiftly restore your consciousness to your physical vessel, thereby impeding any passage through the astral plane. Reposition yourself and venture into the familiar environs nearby and any other locations you may journey to.

11. Record your experiences. After reuniting with your physical form, document the events that occurred. Maintain a personal diary and meticulously record all visual observations, emotional experiences, olfactory perceptions, and other sensory impressions. You might encounter unexpected discoveries during the course of your exploration.

12. Meditate. This method serves as a means to enhance awareness, which I firmly believe is a fundamental aspect for initiating the experience of astral projection. In addition, this will enhance the frequency of lucid dreaming experiences. Above all, it is crucial to note that by enhancing consciousness in the realm of the physical, a similar effect will be observed in the realm of the astral, thereby greatly enhancing the comfort levels of your astral journeys.

Dream Control

Numerous fortuitous occurrences are influenced by one's present mindset, affording you the capability to exert influence over your dreams. In these dream sequences, your astral form shall maintain a consistent forward motion, without halting in the resting area. In subsequent occurrences, it has been discovered that during an astral projection, the individual is able to witness their astral form projected within a dream-like setting upon awakening. Hence, through diligent practice, you will acquire the ability to evoke the intended thought. Dream control pertains to the technique of astral projection and serves as a gratifying modality. On this occasion, X. Carrington asserts the subsequent statement: "An achievable methodology exists for invoking veridical dreams." While transitioning into slumber, it is imperative to discern the manner in which consciousness enters a state of repose.

By engaging in these experiments on oneself, one will gradually attain the capacity to consciously regulate their faculties until the point at which they are fully immersed in slumber. The phenomenon of contemplation of oneself during the state of deep slumber is profoundly intriguing. Once you have acquired the knowledge on how to perform this task, endeavor to construct a vivid mental representation that encompasses a particular scenario, directing your unwavering attention towards it. Subsequently, in the final moments prior to entering a state of dreaming, intentionally and purposefully transition yourself to this visual depiction - in essence, immerse yourself within the depicted scenario. Through diligent self-training, you will acquire the ability to seamlessly transition your consciousness into a state of sleep. And in this way, you will gain an amazing wholeness of thought. There will be a seamless continuity in your consciousness as you immerse yourself in the dream imagery and maintain a conscious awareness of the dream. You are about to experience an authentic reverie that will ensure your recollection of events with utmost precision.

Is Mr. Carrington aware of the remarkable alignment between his instructions pertaining to "authentic dreams" and the techniques employed in dream manipulation to engage the astral form in an otherworldly experience? The initial requirement is to transport the astral body to the location of activity, in accordance with the unspoken concurrence established by the conscious slumber. Once you acquire the ability to encourage the manifestation of positive or beneficial aspects and induce mental imagery, you will be able to successfully initiate the presence of your astral body within a dream state. Consequently, upon awakening, you will either retain full recollection of the experience or find yourself immersed in a state of immersive dreaming. In this scenario, the dream will dissipate, and you will encounter a state of projection.

Know What It Real?

Numerous individuals require the validation of their experiences, particularly in the initial stages. An inquiry frequently encountered upon resumption from an astral projection encounter is, "Did my experience possess veracity?"

One can arrive at an answer to their question by further defining their personal interpretation of reality. Nevertheless, the utmost crucial aspect to contemplate in addressing this inquiry is the degree of authenticity in regards to the impact that the encounter had upon oneself. Did it provide you with genuine healing and provoke meaningful contemplation? If the effects on your well-being and mental state were significant, the factual veracity of the experience becomes inconsequential, would you not agree?

Sharing Your Experiences

Individuals have a strong desire to share their experiences with others upon their initial return. This proclivity bears resemblance to the desire to extensively recount one's experiences and observations during a vacation taken in a tangible location. There is no inherent issue with communicating your experiences to individuals who possess a receptive and encouraging attitude towards your endeavors.

If, in the event that you encounter an instance where someone you desire to communicate with refuses to acknowledge your perspective, it is essential to refrain from internalizing the rejection as a personal affront. Embracing an alternate reality within the realm of spirituality has the potential to profoundly disrupt one's fundamental belief system, and undertaking such transformations is invariably arduous. Should an individual respond unfavorably to your narrative, their reaction speaks more to their own disposition than to your own story. In particular, initially confide only in individuals whom you are certain will respond receptively to your narrative, even if their belief is limited to acknowledging your own conviction in the reality of what transpired.

It is imperative to bear in mind that not all spiritual experiences are intended to be divulged. In the event of a particularly sacred occurrence or when explicitly advised by a spiritual guide or being, it is imperative to display reverence and adhere to the boundary of refraining from disclosing the shared message or encounter. Certain wisdom may be too sophisticated for those who are inexperienced, and acquiring it prematurely could potentially impede their individual pursuits.

In summation, your experience with the return process is expected to be favorable. By cultivating self-compassion, exercising patience, and fostering understanding, one can acquire an abundance of knowledge and personal development through the practice of astral travel. The knowledge you have recently acquired will profoundly enrich your daily existence, ushering in a profound sense of serenity and contentment. Embrace this experience with an open mind, and you will undoubtedly witness positive outcomes. The entire procedure was the opposite of my experience in rising from bed. The specter descended gradually, exhibiting vibrations, and then abruptly plummeted, once more synchronizing with the corporeal form. Every muscle of my physical frame quivered, and an intense sensation of agony permeated my being as if I had been rigorously compressed from head to toe upon the instant of contact. I experienced a revival of my physical being, accompanied by a profound sense of wonder, mingled with trepidation. I maintained consciousness throughout the entirety of the unfolding events.

Following that particular expedition, I have undergone numerous additional projections that have exhibited various divergences from the aforementioned sensations. However, they consistently align with regards to the trajectory of bodily movement that I have just delineated. Despite the commonly held belief that repetition leads to enhanced skills, this initial projection was extraordinarily unique, surpassing the clarity exhibited by many skilled mediums in their best attempts. While I have confidence in my innate ability to visualize, I attribute the uniqueness of this initial manifestation to the presence of multiple extraordinary individuals who were slumbering in an adjoining room to the one I was accommodated in. It is an acknowledged reality within the realm of occult practice that a "line of power" can be forged between individuals, with the intention of conferring advantageous outcomes upon one of them.

Now let's move on. The state of consciousness can be disrupted at any given moment, regardless of the location or specific circumstances surrounding this phenomenon. This phenomenon may manifest as a fluctuation in consciousness, or knowledge may not be engaged in it whatsoever. Typically, in cases where consciousness is implicated, it invariably commences subsequent to the separation and locomotion of the astral body, with individuals remaining completely unaware of this state until the moment of becoming awake. The intervention of consciousness that occurs most frequently is highly preferred. In this instance, the subject's cognizance does not encompass the initial and disagreeable phases, as alluded to in the preceding narrative. The main stages encompass involuntarily induced catalepsy, unpredictable motions, and elevation. These experiences are not pleasurable for the individuals involved, but over time they may develop a desensitization. However, it is worth noting that these initial stages invariably take place during a state of unconsciousness, assuming that the exteriorization is accompanied by the physical body assuming a horizontal orientation."

Physical Manifestation: Interplay Between Sex And Astral Projection

The sexual impulse bears resemblance to any other vital muscular or cerebral function. The greater its usage, the more attuned and refined it becomes. Cease its utilization, and it shall become lax and deteriorate in form. When was the most recent occasion in which you encountered an individual who possesses a sedentary lifestyle but exhibits an exceptional physical physique? Probably never. The identical premise is applicable to the sexual desire. When one prioritizes other commitments, finds themselves in a negative relationship, or experiences exhaustion, their libido may falter, resulting in a diminished sexual drive.

However, allowing one's sexual desire to diminish is not always a deliberate choice. Several factors contribute to the decrease in your sexual desire, such as:

1. Major depressive disorders and their pharmacological treatments

2. Cardiovascular disease, hypertension, neoplastic conditions, diabetes mellitus, and substance abuse.

3. Over-the-counter cold/allergy medications,

4. Hormonal imbalance,

5. Difficulties within the relationship - feelings of resentment towards your partner

6. Smoking/alcohol/illegal drugs,

7. You are unaccompanied,

Furthermore, there are numerous examples to be considered.

Consider the most recent occasion when your libido was significantly diminished.

How did the remainder of your life unfold? Have you observed that the other facets of your life have deteriorated? Did it feel as though you were encountering an insurmountable obstacle regardless of the strategies or methods you employed?

There exist three distinct approaches to initiate an out of body experience:

Upon engaging with another form of energy through any of the three aforementioned manners, one is concurrently engaging in the transfer of energy. A portion of your energy is imparted to them, just as a portion of their energy is transferred to you. Exercise caution when selecting individuals to establish connections with. If you associate with an individual lacking conscientiousness, their energy will assimilate into your own until you undergo an energy purging.

Does engaging in sexual activities outside of a committed relationship constitute infidelity?

This inquiry frequently arises from individuals who find themselves in relationships characterized by a lack of emotional or physical intimacy. If an individual engages in sexual activity with someone other than their partner, would it be regarded as infidelity? Infidelity is perceived differently by each individual involved in a romantic relationship.

Sexual activity within the realm of OBE encompasses an interaction solely at the energetic level, without any form of physical integration. Different individuals perceive the concept of cheating in distinct manners. For certain individuals, it constitutes the disclosure of personal details; for others, it entails the exchange of a kiss, and for a third group, it refers to engaging in sexual intercourse or oral sex. In the context of an intimate relationship with limited sexual activity, engaging in out-of-body experiences (OBEs) can effectively enhance the physical aspect of your sexual life with your partner. The heightened sensations experienced during OBE encounters can significantly stimulate your physical desires, thereby fostering a desire for intimate release with your partner. In a mutually nurturing and harmonious relationship, engaging in OBE sex serves as a complement rather than a substitute, amplifying the intimate connection between partners. In a relationship devoid of love, engaging in OBE sex can potentially rekindle latent emotions and affection between the partners.

The concept of OBE (Out of Body Experience) sex distinctively differs from online and phone sex due to the motivation behind engaging in these activities. Unlike online/phone sex, individuals often opt for this alternative as a means to avoid physical intimacy with their partner. Two individuals situated at distinct positions behind their respective technological devices are engaging in activities aimed at attaining genuine orgasmic experiences.

Each individual who participated in the act of engaging in explicit conversations or interactions with others through electronic devices subsequently expresses a lack of desire to engage in sexual activity with their respective partner. This statement represents solely my perspective. Every individual must arrive at their own conclusion.

White Light Protection

No, contraceptive measures are unnecessary for sexual encounters during out-of-body experiences. I am not referring to that specific form of protection. You require measures to shield yourself from the influence of negative energies depleting your strength and persistently clinging onto you.

To ensure personal safety during an out-of-body experience, it is recommended to envelop oneself in a radiant aura of pure white luminescence. It's easy to do. Kindly shut your eyes and envision the celestial expanse unfurling before you, encompassing your being with a radiant luminescence. Please maintain the image for a brief duration before continuing your journey.

Cultivating Your Inner Radiance

Prior to embarking on the quest for OBE encounters, it is advisable to undertake measures in order to enhance or fortify one's inner luminosity. The internal flame is indeed synonymous with our essence. The justification for the necessity of its reinforcement lies in the fact that despite its initial radiance at the moment of birth, our soul inevitably becomes burdened by copious layers of negativity over the course of our lives. Phrases such as, "I will spend the remainder of my existence in solitude," "I possess an unwelcome excess of body mass," or "I will fail to achieve any substantial accomplishments."

Each time a disparaging remark is made, the radiance within us becomes tarnished. We are making it more difficult to shine through the self-imposed crap pile.

In situations where the illumination of your inner light is diminished, it is more likely that you will encounter energies of a lower vibrational frequency during your out-of-body experiences. I will discuss the concept of disseminating personal authority. When engaging in intimate activity with another person, whether it involves out-of-body experiences or physical intercourse, the energies of both individuals become intermingled. Hence, it is imperative to maintain a heightened and resilient energy vibration, thereby ensuring that you solely draw individuals of a higher vibrational resonance into your sphere.

Experiences Of Astral Projection

A significant quantity of psychic energy is generated or assimilated, both within an extensive external encounter and within lucid dreams. It is also contingent upon the particular form of energy.

This force can manifest as a relentless vigor that imparts the sensation of remaining awake for extended periods, vigorously obliterating obstacles and embracing the entire world. Alternatively, it can be a subdued and imperceptible strength discreetly accumulated for deployment at a later, opportune moment, such as a momentous occasion on the imminent horizon.

The second entity possesses the capabilities of flight, nocturnal vision, and teleportation, to provide a few illustrations. However, tasks such as providing sustenance, quenching his thirst, and facilitating access through doors are beyond his capabilities. In the subsequent lengthy encounter, of which only a segment will be delineated herein, there exists an autonomous cognitive entity intrinsic to the dream realm, manifesting as an observably perceptive educational encounter...

I awakened during the nocturnal hours and encountered difficulty in repositioning myself laterally. Upon prompt realization, it became evident to me that I had not yet transitioned back to my primary physical form, as my second body was still in the process of reuniting with it. Consequently, I successfully apprehended it. I allowed myself to unwind and concentrated on gradually releasing tension, until I assumed an upright posture within the confines of the room.

Following my success, I proceeded to observe my hands. They retained their natural skin tone, albeit with a degree of transparency. I would be able to examine them and observe the impact on my carpet.

In summary, I initially believed that my hands possessed this particular design, although it turned out that they were merely translucent. Subsequently, I proceeded a short distance towards the balcony and contemplated the possibility of simply traversing the doorway. Upon doing so, the entire scene underwent a transformation. I had instantaneously transported myself to an alternate setting.

Abruptly, I discovered that I was situated within what resembled a subterranean chamber.

Adjacent to me was an aged gentleman, with whom I had encountered on numerous occasions through visions or astral journeys, and who engaged in conversation with me. He instructed me to diligently observe everything in the ensuing minutes, emphasizing the importance of not overlooking any detail.

I examined everything with precision. A lengthy table was situated in the vicinity of his position. There were a pair of youthful individuals grasping darts within their hands. There was a candle placed upon the table, casting its luminous glow upon the room. Notably, there lacked any alternative source of light, particularly considering the absence of any discernible windows. Additionally, a timepiece was present within the confines of the room.

One of the boys approached the edge of the table and intended to align the dart with the clock positioned on the table. It appeared as though he directed his aim and executed a throw. After being tossed three times, the elderly gentleman nodded in approval and appeared satisfied. Subsequently, his gaze shifted towards me. Therefore, I rose from my seat, walked toward the periphery of the table, picked up the three darts in question, and directed my attention towards the target. The candle was positioned on the right side of the clock.

Therefore, as I was carefully aligning my shot, the elderly gentleman suddenly leapt to his feet and extinguished the candle with a gust of air.

That elicited a strong surge of anger within me. I harbored a strong belief that his actions were mere attempts to intimidate me, as the subtle fluctuations of the candle flame allowed for precise determination of the wind's origin and consequently facilitated more accurate targeting than my predecessor.

Therefore, I had to manage without this assistance and instead directed my attention towards the rectangular, ivory-colored timepiece adorned with black numerals and hands. The crimson-colored second hand was observed, while the objective appeared to be a distance of approximately two meters from its current position. With a slight snap, I took aim and threw.

Abruptly, the man leapt to his feet and hurriedly approached me. Instantly, I discerned his utter discontentment with me. Frightened, I woke up.

Upon regaining consciousness in my physical form, I promptly documented this occurrence; however, initially, I did not contemplate the peculiar conclusion. It was only recently when I came to the realization that I finally understood the reason behind the man's disappointment in me. He extinguished the candle, whereupon I appropriated the sole illumination available. Nevertheless, despite the absence of light, I remained capable of discerning the precise position of the clock.

I failed to observe this fact; instead, it spurred the emergence of a veil that attempted to distort the true purpose of the candle in my perception. It became evident at that point: as soon as the gentleman extinguished the candle, I immediately discerned through the vision of the secondary entity, which possesses exceptional sight capabilities in low-light conditions. Regrettably, I was unable to bring this fact to my attention due to my own lack of intelligence.

The element of intelligence lay in the premise that the dream encounter ought to impart knowledge, yet regrettably, my own intellectual capacity surpassed this requirement - a fact evident in this particular instance.

In my personal opinion, there were two potential viewpoints during that period: Either this dream was orchestrated by a superior intellect aiming to impart knowledge on utilizing its secondary form, or it transitioned from an external encounter to a state of lucid dreaming, wherein the ability to perceive visuals in darkness is likewise feasible. Ultimately, I concluded that the distinction between an astral journey and a lucid dream may not be crucial, for the undeniable reality remains that I failed to realize my innate ability to perceive in the darkness of that realm. It is evident that our dreams and related experiences are under the control of a superior intellect.

Analogous incidents can be observed in alternative contexts. As an illustration, the transition from an out of body experience (OBE) to a more akin to a dreamlike state can be described as a envisaged, disembodied encounter (TAKE). This implies that one has the opportunity to aspire to encounter an external encounter.

After achieving a state of relaxation, I gained composure and found myself in my room. I promptly surveyed my surroundings and assessed whether everything was as per normal. My physical form was resting within the confines of the bed, devoid of any foreign entities that were not meant to be present. Therefore, I proceeded to the window of my balcony and simply strolled through it.

While traversing the area, I discerned a temporary impression: a notable alteration had occurred. It encompassed not only my fundamental disposition, but also my cognitive interpretation. It can be likened to a brief moment of blackout, characterized by an unobtrusive and nearly imperceptible transition.

It appeared as though all functionalities ceased to operate, resembling a dissociative episode. Upon surveying my surroundings, I noticed that the balcony window behind me presented a stark contrast to my customary view. Additionally, I observed the presence of additional balconies to both my left and right. In summary, I proceeded to one of the alternate balconies whereupon I gazed through the window.

I observed an individual reclining in their bed, in a state of slumber, though their alternate form remained concealed from view. Upon my visual observation of the balcony, I discerned the presence of an individual occupying a seat at a table. He appeared noticeably despondent, prompting me to approach him and engage in conversation. Upon inspecting his quarters, I contemplated the notion that were it to belong to a neighboring individual, it would be improbable to observe such meticulous tidiness.

Upon awakening, I immediately discerned that the shift from reality to a dream state had occurred at the precise instant following my passage through the door leading to the balcony. An absence of attentiveness and a disruption in the flow of consciousness had occurred.

Despite still feeling detached from reality afterwards, it is likely that the experience seamlessly transitioned into a dream or perhaps I had been transported to another location, as is often the case in such states.

In this context, I would also like to present several instances recounted by an acquaintance who likewise underwent episodes of disembodiment and encountered significant challenges related to apprehensions: "

I regained consciousness while I was in the confines of my restroom. It was evident that I had a distinct sensation of being detached from my physical self, which instilled a mild sense of fear in me. Therefore, I hastily sprinted with the intention of returning to my physical form, which lay motionless in my sleeping quarters. Upon initiating movement towards the exit, my physical senses were already fully conscious.

During the nocturnal hours, I regained consciousness and promptly comprehended my state of disembodiment. Nonetheless, I lacked the audacity to rise and move about, therefore I remained reclined in bed and intermittently raised either my left or right arm solely for observation. It dawned upon me that it briefly exhibited transparency before returning to its usual appearance. I pursued this endeavor for a period of time, until I regained consciousness.

Next:

I reclined upon the bed, rendered immobile, as if operating within my second physical form. Subsequently, I experienced potent vibrations, or mildly discomforting vibrations, coursing through my entire body.

Simultaneously, I became aware of a resonant and somber sound emanating. The dissociation from my physical form occurred effortlessly. As I levitated at a distance of approximately half a meter above my corporeal form, I made the conscious decision to return. However, due to my lack of knowledge regarding the methods to bring both bodies together, I instead focused my efforts on mobilizing my prominent right toe, which promptly resulted in my awakening.

Next:

Upon awakening during the nocturnal hours and observing the impending departure of my consciousness from my physical being, profound sensations of solitude and mortality overwhelmed me. The initial endeavors to achieve detachment posed a challenge to me, but I ultimately triumphed, resulting in the elimination of fear.

In my viewpoint, these enduring anxieties are connected to apprehension regarding mortality. Numerous individuals who have undergone near-death experiences commonly recount instances of disassociation from the corporeal form. This phenomenon may give rise to an innate sense of apprehension that alters one's disposition and endeavors to impede the occurrence of an out-of-body encounter as a mere act of self-preservation. It is imperative to cultivate one's determination and fortitude.

Only individuals who overcome their fears and undergo an out-of-body experience truly have the ability to perceive it. For instance, an illustrative experience that aids in emphasizing the aforementioned point is the following:

I eventually sought to partake in an out of body phenomenon, yet consistently encountered an obstacle at the moment when my physical form achieved utmost relaxation; as soon as my mind desired it, my cranial sensation grew exponentially, causing apprehension of potential rupture.

After a brief passage of time, the magnitude of the pressure became so overwhelming that I terminated the engagement. However, it was perhaps on my tenth endeavor that I consciously acknowledged my readiness to embrace all circumstances. I became resolute, accepting the sole accountability for whether I would achieve liberation from the confines of my physical existence or face the potential consequence of mental implosion.

Subsequently, the intensity of the pressure became overwhelmingly burdensome to the point where I momentarily surmised that he might actually rupture, yet unexpectedly, the pressure dissipated. Subsequently, I experienced an astounding sense of physical relaxation, which confirmed that I had taken a significant stride forward.

In the subsequent encounter, I would like to bring focus to an energetic phenomenon that impedes my state of detachment:

I reclined on my sleeping surface and perceived the oscillations, once again resonating within my auditory receptacles. Subsequently, I observed that these oscillations emanate from the corporeal form and generate a vertically oriented, funnel-shaped energy field, thereby hindering my ability to regulate my secondary entity. Therefore, I was compelled to remove myself from my current path in order to elude this particular domain. Therefore, I shifted my position and subsequently found myself able to rise effortlessly.

This unique "domain" appeared to be composed of energy, as no alternative notion comes to mind that could more effectively depict it. The field operates, in my estimation, akin to an elevator, wherein it either ensnares the secondary body and subsequently joins it with the corporeal body, or conversely, ascends it and maintains it within orbit - a phenomenon perceived as rapid velocity in the aforementioned encounters.

Unplanned instances of detachment from the physical body, accompanied by a fundamental sense of safety, consistently yield highly exhilarating, entertaining, and enlightening occurrences.

With remarkable speed, I disengaged from my physical form and found myself in the confines of my bedroom. Raising my arm with intent, I initiated the sensation of soaring through the air. Without delay, I ascended from the ground and propelled upwards, piercing through the ceiling towards the heavens. In that moment, my mind was momentarily stimulated, and I entertained the notion of embarking on a journey to Asia.

Upon a delightful journey above majestic peaks, amidst billowy vapors, and traversing verdant woodlands and picturesque valleys, I arrived at a vast expanse of land.

Some women were present, sporting oversized straw hats of circular shape. I perceived a slight sense of annoyance within me and subsequently descended, gracefully gliding above the expanse of the field. As I approached her, I fervently and expeditiously rotated them. I was taken aback by the fact that even my screams were audible to them, as I generally went unnoticed in other circumstances.

One of the ladies consistently maintained her gaze towards my direction. It seemed as though she possessed a partial glimpse of my presence. Her gaze tracked the movement, but subsequently she swiftly departed. A short time later, she came back with a brownish sack, and when I slammed her to scare her again, she reached into her sack and took out a severed pig's head.

He appeared to be covered in blood, which filled me with fear, prompting me to swiftly retreat back into my physical vessel and awaken.

Upon awakening, I found myself wearing a wry smile, as it became evident that I had been under scrutiny for allegedly being a malevolent entity that posed a threat to their crops, resulting in my inevitable banishment akin to that of any other miscreant. It had exhibited an impact, as I was promptly thrust backward upon encountering a decapitated, sanguine swine head directly in my line of sight.

I consistently resorted to making such jests in the absence of more compelling alternatives, and invariably derived immense delight from doing so. On occasion, I would visit unfamiliar abodes or inconvenienced individuals I came across while journeying.

Frequently, I would come across inhabited abodes, as the inhabitant may have been journeying alone, presumably devoid of recollection the following day. There is indeed no law enforcement authority that possesses the power to prohibit either option, and this fact itself grants us an extraordinary degree of freedom, especially within a society that has enacted numerous statutes, wherein even the most upright individuals find themselves to some extent inherently inclined towards transgression.

Many principles and teachings commonly express that an individual must possess great love, absence of guilt, and complete solitude in their pursuit of goodness, light, and love in order to attain an out-of-body experience.

Certainly, I can envision a scenario where an individual, such as a murderer, might encounter challenges in traversing to an astral plane due to underlying psychological barriers and apprehensions related to confronting their victims and grappling with their own subconscious and emotions. However, it generally holds true that any individual, regardless of their background, intellectual capacity, or moral compass, should possess the inherent capability to access this realm independently. The lack of compliance with this requirement may stem from factors such as limited understanding, doubt, an overly analytical mindset, as well as a general lack of enthusiasm towards attaining these circumstances.

Individuals who assert that a visit to said states is only feasible for those who have obtained profound understanding, in accordance with the information at my disposal, clearly diverge from verifiable realities. Every individual engages in astral travel on a nightly basis, irrespective of their recollection thereof. This is pertinent to both children and larger animals.

One does not require expertise, initiation, or mastery to excel in this art. In fact, one must possess a significant amount of patience, motivation, and dedication to practice.

Additional occurrences may likewise transpire during an instance of disembodiment, such as visual or auditory phenomena. Not solely within the realm of disengagement, wherein electronic sounds are frequently discerned, but also throughout the entirety of the encounter:

Upon regaining consciousness, I found myself in my alternate physical form within the confines of my personal sleeping quarters, albeit in a different resting spot. Upon inspection, I noticed that my living quarters were brimming with items I had previously disposed of, in addition to those that remained in my possession. Even the impaired or flawed items appeared to have endured in their previous positions. They remained stationary and continued to perform their duties without any damage or disruption. However, there were also unrecognized objects present. I was astonished by the considerable occupancy of the room. Upon making contact with the object, a fleeting luminosity manifested itself discreetly at the tips of my fingers. Intrigued, I proceeded to make contact with the wall.

It seemed as though a fire crackled against a wall, emitting radiant sparks. It unequivocally originated from my second entity, of which I now had substantial certainty. Hence, I possessed an invaluable duplicate physical form.

I chuckled, as the recollection of a friend's comment crossed my mind. They had bestowed upon me the moniker of "Golden Jonah" due to my previous account of a comparable incident wherein I traversed a staircase and observed an intriguing, luminous glow that persistently coexisted with my presence. It was only later that I discerned this radiance emanated from my very own astral form.

I pondered the possibility of each individual possessing a distinctive hue. The color black would have been more fitting for me, as it provides a measure of anonymity. However, I must admit that the golden hue also presents a pleasing aesthetic. I observed an object of dimensions comparable to that of a hand, which happened to be a pale, Indian elephant. I applied pressure with my finger onto his ocular region, and to my astonishment, it emitted a gleaming golden hue, indicating that the eye had come to life. Its composition subsequently transformed into a synthetic material, exhibiting the sudden emergence of a discernible pupil and intricate iris.

Upon surveying my surroundings, I observed that after I made contact with my finger once more, the situation returned to its previous state of normalcy. I discovered that my second corporeal form possessed the extraordinary ability to restore objects to life, filling me with immense fascination. I came into contact with various objects, and they consistently exhibited liveliness in response to my presence. I experienced a sense of immense power and authority. On occasion, I hurriedly moved alongside the wall in order to catch a glimpse of the cascading golden sparks. It was very impressive.

Nonetheless, there exist countless out-of-body experiences that are less cognizant and exhilarating in nature, thereby lacking the complete engagement of an individual:

During the night, I remained awake and perceived the sensation of being in a reclined position. I extended my hand towards it and observed that a coil from the mattress had become dislodged. I exerted force upon it to suppress it, but it did not dissipate. I assumed an altered bodily posture and sought to attend to it on a separate occasion. Upon my previous observation, I did not witness the presence of a displaced feather.

Despite being in a state of disembodiment, it is likely that I possessed the ability to perceive sensations emanating from the bed, such as the movement of the mattress springs. Due to this rationale, I surmised that the mattress had incurred damage and devised a short-sighted plan to repair or replace it.

Recurring instances of comparable nature will continuously manifest themselves to you, wherein you remain largely oblivious to your state...

Throughout the duration, I had been bothered incessantly by a mosquito, prompting my sudden action to swiftly illuminate the surroundings and apprehend the insect. I cautiously explored the dimly-lit surroundings, methodically seeking out the switch to illuminate the room. I applied pressure to it with the intention of activating the light, yet it failed to respond. Upon tapping once more and experiencing another lack of response, I contemplated within myself that this state of affairs would undoubtedly be of limited duration, after which the luminosity would inevitably cease. Subsequently, I proceeded towards the window with the intention of closing it in order to eliminate any further presence of mosquitoes.

This phenomenon can be regarded as a quintessential example of an out of body experience, characterized by a state of reduced self-awareness and the likelihood of a subsequent encounter with the practitioner.

A few of my encounters encompassed an entirely novel facet that I acquired knowledge about only several years later. I consistently found myself awakening within a darkened chamber, the precise nature of which eluded my discernment.

Last night, I retired to my bed and endeavored to resolve my state of mind by employing a different approach wherein I simulated slumber. I hypothesized that within altered states of consciousness, particularly the realm of my subconscious mind, determining the veracity of my state of wakefulness would prove to be challenging. So I feigned slumber.

This had a conspicuous impact, as a fragment of my being appeared to instantaneously endorse this notion. It swiftly circulated in my vicinity, prompting me to adopt an intense state of focus, while simultaneously maintaining the facade of slumber.

Abruptly, the initial alteration occurred, causing an instantaneous loss of bodily sensation. I experienced a strong sense of gravity within my own physical being. I can assure you that it is extremely soothing. I was already familiar with this state, as it closely resembles a disconnection from the physical form.

In an instant thereafter, I found myself ensconced once more within an abyss of blackness, perceiving solely the rustling of the wind that brushed against my hair. It appeared to me as though I were hurtling through the inky expanse of night with remarkable velocity. Subsequently, I experienced a sudden relinquishing of command over my physical vessel, as I gently levitated rearward and continued to soar for a brief duration, until ultimately reintegrating with my corporeal form.

The occurrence of this darkness and the palpable breeze that rustles through my hair has frequently crossed my mind, consistently presenting me with enigmatic questions. I pondered the potential of the world and contemplated my own existence...

Throughout the entirety of the night, which encompassed a relatively brief period from approximately 03:00 to 06:00am, my experiences were primarily marked by occurrences of disembodied states. I resided concurrently in multiple apartments, alternating between their respective beds, thereby experiencing a constant state of transition and frequent changes of residence. I encountered various instances wherein I reclined on the bed, yet the surroundings and the bed itself were consistently distinct.

Once, I accompanied a female acquaintance to a nursery school, where it appeared as though we remained for a considerable period of time. In the dimly lit surroundings, I conveyed to her my expectation of undergoing a recurring experience, specifically referring to the sudden separation of my consciousness from my corporeal form.

I glided gracefully across the room once more until I found myself instantaneously transported to another location. Subsequently, I reclined upon a raised bed resembling a loft, and it was in this setting that the distance I maintained from surroundings brought about the most efficient outcome. I was readily able to disengage from my physical form and levitate within the confines of the room, but regrettably, my vision remained devoid of any perceivable stimuli.

In the interim, I engaged in swift aerial movement. I was thoroughly astonished as, upon attaining velocity, a gentle breeze coincided instantaneously, augmenting or diminishing proportionally to my flight velocity. I experienced the sensation of airborne travel, with the wind streaming through my hair akin to the act of leaning one's head outside a moving vehicle. The entire duration of the experience is estimated to have been nearly two hours.

It is unnecessary for one to consider that I had been deprived of three hours of sleep. In fact, such occurrences are notably more invigorating than a typical night's rest. The physical body maintains its regular and customary state of slumber during instances of lucid dreaming or out-of-body encounters. The disparity primarily lies in the level of consciousness or memory retention achieved during such an experience...

Once more, I regained consciousness in my secondary form and glided through the abyss, sensing the well-known and delightful impetus."

After an extensive period of flight, I found myself questioning my geographic location. I relished the sensation until I reunited my consciousness with my physical form.

While I was occupied with wakefulness within my resting place and contemplating the event, I subsequently underwent a transition back to my secondary physical form. I navigated swiftly through this profound darkness following the separation, until I suddenly beheld the vast expanse of space.

Was I present throughout the entirety of a region within the universe, perceptibly devoid of stars? Regardless, I experienced a sense of gratification upon encountering something once more. Subsequently, I arrived at a temple that appeared to be situated in the midst of space, positioned on a plateau of sorts.

I touched down on the temple's courtyard. The stone comprising the temple exhibited a brownish hue, and all elements within were fashioned from this material. Before me was an imposing staircase, which I ascended swiftly. Within the confines of the structure, there existed several chambers; however, these spaces were consistently devoid of furnishings or ornamentation. Afterward, I found myself back in the forecourt, positioned myself at the precipice, and embarked on a plunge into the void. In that instant, darkness engulfed my surroundings once more, and I was carried back by the well-known gusts, until I eventually regained consciousness.

In this dark emptiness, subsequently referred to as the "Void," I detailed an existence detached from the confines of the system, devoid of any perception save for that of its own presence. There is no danger present, nor has anyone been apprehended. The state of "Void" is, without question, an exceedingly tranquil experience, provided one is adept at savouring it.

Undoubtedly, there remains a considerable amount of territory to be investigated pertaining to this phenomenon of the second body, along with the potentialities it presents. Though challenging, once one has overcome obstacles and desires to embark on an adventurous journey, it is not a simple task. Conducting research typically occurs unintentionally solely in the presence of challenges.

Alternatively, in the event that circumstances transpire favorably and the predicament is resolved effortlessly, the child becomes awakened and thereby encounters unplanned occurrences in which one may soar freely. The sensation of existing beyond one's physical self can be likened to an experience of euphoria, liberation, and exploration.

Furthermore, these emotions exert an influence on the psyche in a manner that dissuades one from engaging in mundane examinations. I had previously made diligent endeavors to observe daily existence through the perspective of the electric body and establish correlations; nevertheless, once I found myself detached from the physical form, my attention towards it had completely waned. I would prefer to traverse the skies and partake in thrilling exploits. On only rare occasions did I have the opportunity to conduct examinations, such as observing a smartphone from the lens of electrical conductivity or similar phenomena.

Yesterday, I had slept until 08:30 pm, as I had retired to bed around 05:00 p.m. Consequently, I intended to avail myself of this opportunity to return to bed no later than 1:00 a.m., in order to establish an ideal state conducive to the separation of my physical body.

After approximately thirty minutes had elapsed, I successfully transitioned to my alternate physical form using a novel technique that I had recently unearthed. Notwithstanding these circumstances, I had to embark on further movement in order to rise from bed. Subsequently, I positioned myself beside my bed and subsequently proceeded towards the doorway of the bedroom.

Upon entering the threshold, I immediately found myself within an unfamiliar abode. I inadvertently relocated once more. However, as I pondered, I grew intrigued by the location to which my elevated consciousness had once again transported me.

I found myself in an unfamiliar living space. In that location, an acquaintance from the past was seated on a sofa, engrossed in a television program as he partook in lighthearted activities. After discreetly coughing, I caught his attention.

He was significantly alarmed:

"What... May I inquire as to the means by which you arrived at this location? You now reside in Freiburg, and unexpectedly, you find yourself in my abode during the late hours of the night?

"I had intended to pay you a visit..." I uttered, with a light-hearted chuckle.

It comes as no surprise that he was perturbed, given that we resided at a considerable distance of several hundred miles from each other. To my astonishment, he managed to discern my presence.

In the subsequent moment, I found myself in a state of ambiguity as to whether it was possible for me to render my presence discernible in this location, if I so desired, or if he too was inhabiting his secondary form in a state of unconsciousness.

Subsequently, we glided briefly in unison, and to his astonishment, he remained taken aback by how effortlessly I engaged in a dive within the confines of his parlor.

"I strongly recommend opting for the Astral Test as it stands out as the optimal choice." I proposed.

Could you please identify this object and provide a description of its intended appearance?"

I accompanied him to the entrance of one of the rooms. We advanced towards it, and I conveyed, 'We can ascertain our whereabouts upon accessing this entrance, determining the physical vessel in which we presently reside.'

Subsequently, I extended my hand through the entrance, which resulted in my hand traversing into the interior. However, upon withdrawing it, I noticed a slight elongation.

I must clarify that while it is evident that I am not in possession of my physical form, I do indeed inhabit an alternate corporeal vessel. It is now your opportunity to act."

Furthermore, he extended his hand through the door and encountered similar difficulty in extracting it. Consequently, he arrived at the identical deduction.

I must say, it appears that you are a golem," I remarked, wearing an amused expression on my face.

"A golem? He inquired in response, "Could you please clarify the meaning of that?"

"This is what I call people who do what they do in their physical body, without knowing that they are in their second body. You appear to be an individual who is not conscious of the fact that you are engaged in traveling. It can be argued that the portrayal of travellers might be exaggerated..."

Ah, I comprehend! I reclined upon the sofa and engaged in the act of viewing the television, albeit in my ethereal form, thus mistaking it for a physical experience."

"Right, that's it!"

Am I to understand that I will be reclining in the bed and engaging in sleep?

I nodded.

"Can I retain this information until the moment I awaken tomorrow?" he inquired.

"No, probably not..."

"Pity...", he countered. "This is such an exciting experience and I will forget it again..."

This holds true for all Golems. I informed him that they venture out during the night to locations where they find happiness in daylight as well, engaging in activities they typically partake in throughout the entire day.

Abruptly, we perceived voices resonating through the corridor. An individual had entered through the main entrance. Collectively, we embarked on a joint expedition. We encountered a female and a male individual at that location. The woman donned a trouser suit, while the man sported a blue overall.

"The purpose of our visit today is to assess the heating system and address the concerns that you raised last week," the lady elaborated. He inquired, "What is the reason behind their ability to perceive our presence?" Subsequently, we exchanged glances, prompting eruptions of boisterous laughter...

Out of body experiences exude a significantly more authentic ambiance compared to that of a lucid dream. For numerous individuals, a clear and vivid dream holds paramount significance, with out-of-body experiences being considered of lesser importance, while certain individuals make a discernment between the two. From a personal standpoint, I too differentiate, as there seems to be no justifiable rationale for harboring the aspiration to supplant one's corporeal form with a more ethereal counterpart.

Additionally, there exists a notable distinction between the phenomena and the laws. An out-of-body experience possesses a narrower scope of manipulation compared to that of a lucid dream. The latter option provides virtually boundless influence, affording the capacity to manipulate everything according to one's desires. Conversely, within an out of body experience, one assumes the role of a passive spectator and observer, journeying to various locations inaccessible in ordinary life and engaging with individuals who are similarly detached from their physical forms. Hence, the assertion of actuality holds significantly increased magnitude and encompasses a wider scope. In a state of heightened awareness during a dream, one encounters divergent realms and engages in activities that are inaccessible in typical, mundane existence.

Mastering Lucid Dreams

In order to acquire the ability to regulate lucid dreams, it is imperative to first develop the skill of discerning one's state of dreaming. It proves to be a considerable challenge to discern between a dream and an actual life occurrence. Nevertheless, once the realization of being in a dream state occurs, one gains the ability to exert control over all unfolding events. Below are several indicators that will allow you to discern whether you are in a dreaming state, thus enabling you to initiate the process of exerting control over the dream (known as lucid dreaming):

Regular prompts to reinforce your awareness of being awake.

Throughout the duration of daylight, it is advisable to ensure that you consistently retain the awareness that you are not in a state of dreaming. An example would be when proceeding towards your vehicle or engaging in a conversation with your employer, you may express, "this reality is not a figment of my imagination." This is an undeniable truth. By practicing this consistently, you will effortlessly discern when you are experiencing a dream. It is advisable to consistently reiterate that assertion prior to entering a state of slumber.

Once an individual embarks on the journey of indulging in their dreams, they will perpetually echo and reinforce that particular assertion. Consequently, you will commence scrutinizing for indications that the unfolding events are indeed fictitious. In the event that you observe peculiar occurrences, it is readily apparent that one is experiencing a dream state. Pose these inquiries to yourself: Are you acquainted with each individual featured in the dream? Have you ever had the opportunity to experience that residence or location within your dreams? Have you had the opportunity to behold the surrounding landscape that is currently within your view? If one is unfamiliar with the individuals, the location, and the surrounding vistas, it is highly likely that one is in a state of reverie or fantasy.

Regular assessments of reality.

Additionally, employing reality checks can aid in determining whether one is experiencing a state of dreaming or not. As an illustration, one may direct their attention to their hands or legs in order to observe the ensuing occurrences. In the realm of dreams, the majority of things tend to exhibit an inherent vagueness and visual blurriness. One will experience a lack of visibility in regard to their lower extremities and upper appendages. Additionally, you may also consider applying gentle pressure to your skin as a means of determining whether or not you will experience the sensation of discomfort. If one is unable to perceive the sensation of pain, there is a likelihood that they are immersed in a state of reverie.

In the event that you are situated in the sitting room, it is advisable to meticulously evaluate the furnishings present within the space. Has everything been arranged in its customary placement? In the event that certain items within the room have undergone displacement, it is plausible to conclude that you are entranced within a dream-like state, unless said items were purposefully rearranged by yourself during the preceding daylight hours.

Direct your attention to your present environment.

It is imperative to consistently ensure a comprehensive comprehension of one's immediate environment and establish a precise awareness of one's whereabouts. If you find yourself situated at a considerable distance from your initial location, endeavor to ascertain the manner in which you arrived there. If you happen to be situated in Paris presently, ponder these inquiries: what was the means by which you arrived there? At what time did you arrive at that location? Was the trip prearranged? When do you plan to return to your residence? May I inquire about the individual who accompanied you on your recent journey? What is the current status of your employment and familial situation? Typically, the ability to respond to these inquiries is diminished during the state of dreaming. To put it differently, the cumulative effect of all the events will be negligible.

For instance, you will find it challenging to ascertain the precise means by which you reached Paris. Upon recognizing the inconsistencies, one can infer that they are in a state of dreaming.

- Monitor and document your patterns and routines.

It is advisable to maintain a diary in close proximity to your bed at all times. Upon immediate awakening, make a written note documenting the contents of your recent dream experience. Strive to apprehend an ample amount of particulars. This course of action will assist you in recollecting your dreams. Over time, one will observe that their dreams and patterns of sleep exhibit a repetitive nature.

As an illustration, the majority of your dreams may occur within a designated urban or rural setting. Additionally, it can be noted that your dreams incorporate your preferred actor, despite the fact that you have yet to encounter them in person. Upon acquiring an awareness of these recurring patterns, one can readily discern the state of being in a dream. For example, upon envisioning a scenario where your beloved actor extends an invitation to his residence, it becomes readily apparent that this occurrence is merely a product of the dream realm.

This is due to your informed understanding that you have never encountered him, thus rendering it implausible that he extended an invitation to you. You are also aware that the majority of your dreams revolve around said actor.

▪ Employ lighting techniques to facilitate the occurrence of lucid dreams

Additionally, one could employ alarm systems that are based on light, allowing for the ability to discern if one is experiencing a state of dreaming. Acquire the aforementioned alarm and subsequently configure it to activate between the durations of four to seven hours. Additionally, it is possible to configure the alarm to activate 4 hours after initial activation, and subsequently repeat every 30 minutes thereafter.

Rather than rousing you from slumber, this alarm will serve as an indicator that you are in the midst of a dream. Extensive research indicates that these alarms exhibit greater efficacy compared to sound-based alarm systems. The alarm will indicate the occurrence of dreaming during the rapid eye movement (REM) phase.

One could utilize a thin sheet to obscure the alarm, thus preventing the light emitted from being excessively luminous and disrupting one's sleep. Keep in mind that your objective is to achieve awareness of being in a dream, rather than to initiate awakening.

Instructions For Attaining

Step One: Dream Recall

For this purpose, it is recommended to maintain a Dream Diary. This holds great significance and can be articulated through a majority of the subsequent procedures. Acquire the following items for your personal use: a large notepad of A4 (foolscap) paper, a brand-new pen, and a supplementary light source such as a side lamp or flashlight, if not already in possession. It is customary to have a hoop binder for conveniently inserting the paper, in this case, the Dream Diary. additionally a nightstand. Arrange all items surrounding your bed in a manner such that they remain easily accessible within arm's length from your usual sleeping position.

Now, proceed to slumber in the usual manner, while keeping this crucial notion in your consciousness: upon awakening, promptly record the contents of your recent reveries. Note the stress. You may potentially awaken for a brief duration during the night, or several hours prior to your usual awakening time, and you might feel inclined, as a result of drowsiness, to remain in a motionless state. DON'T. You should make it a practice to wake up promptly and record, in your dream journal, the thoughts and images that were occupying your mind while you were in slumber.

Even if you can only recall vague particulars, it is advisable to diligently document as much as possible regarding these elusive particulars. In the event that you are unable to recall something, it is advised to document the following statement: "I consciously made the decision to not retain knowledge of my dreams." Please be mindful of the specific phrasing used: you are acknowledging that it is your personal obligation to remember your dreams, and asserting that the ability to recall your dreams lies within your own control – a fact that holds true.

On the subsequent evening, replicate the process. Consistently employ an up-to-date page within your dream journal for each successive night, ensuring that the date is distinctly indicated.

Continuously perform this task no less than once every week. Initially, you will find yourself scarcely prepared to compose even a single sentence encompassing the substance of your dreams. On subsequent evenings, you will be prepared to engage in writing with greater depth and elaboration. Strive consistently to meticulously record every possible detail. Ideally, you should be able to revisit your journal subsequently, such as after returning from work in the evening, and accurately recall the specific unfolding of your dream.

Second step: An introductory overview of Coueism.

This method can be employed to enhance the level of your performance, and can also be utilized to elevate the overall quality of your existence, by establishing a beneficial affirmation for yourself. The author of Bardon's "Initiation into Hermetics" proposes a similar approach, as discerning readers may recall.

Coueism entails employing a strategic approach to transform these desires into subliminal suggestions. "Emile Coue, the original architect behind this technique, established these fundamental principles: Firstly, rephrase the desire as if you were articulating a constructive situation in the present, for instance:

The subsequent action subsequent to making the decision to proceed with the Affirmation involves the repetition of the chosen affirmation twenty times to oneself as one prepares to retire for the night at the stroke of midnight. Coue chose a set of twenty solely due to the fact that, based on his ongoing experiments, it appeared to be the most fitting and appropriate number. The declaration should be sustained when one is on the verge of falling asleep – and again upon awakening when one still feels drowsy.

The underlying rationale behind the effectiveness of Coueism resides in its classification as a psychological condition. The moment of experiencing drowsiness is akin to entering a state of trance, wherein the faculties of the conscious mind are temporarily deactivated and the subconscious becomes highly open to suggestions.

During the process of selecting an affirmation, it is advisable to avoid the inclusion of words that possess dual or ambiguous meanings. The reasoning behind this is that the notion of being unconscious, in opposition to the perspective of thinkers such as Jacques Lacan, does not function in a similar manner as language; rather, it is solely the realm of the conscious mind that operates accordingly. what's going to typically happen is that rather it'll choose words apparently every which way from your Affirmation, and link them with pictures and ideas in your memory with that the individual words are associated.

Step 3: Employing Directed Dreaming Strategies

Once you have attained the ability to recollect your dreams with great detail and are satisfied with the efficacy of Coueism, you may proceed to deliberate upon the substance of your dreams prior to retiring for the night. Below are three recommended strategies to consider: allocate a minimum of one week actively implementing each of them. Subsequently, once you have acquired proficiency, you will possess the ability to independently determine your preference, although to attain optimum proficiency, it is imperative to be proficient in all three.

Procedure A: the fundamental procedure

Select a topic regarding your ideal entity that can be encapsulated within a single sentence. Alternatively, a more elevated option would be to utilize a solitary term. As a novice, opt for a topic where you typically do not exhibit emotion or one that does not typically cross your mind (reserve the experimentation with subjects you are personally involved in for when you have gained more expertise). However, this may present numerous options for you to consider, such as venturing to a distant location, interacting with a renowned individual or historical figure, engaging in an unfamiliar activity, and so forth.

It is prudent for both novices and experienced individuals to adopt an approach towards their pursuit of their dream-work that mirrors the scientific method, namely one characterized by objectivity and detachment. What I intend to convey is that we should approach our pursuit of dreams with a level of dedication and precision similar to how we would expect scientists to approach their experiments. While many researchers are often motivated by the monetary value of patent rights and the recognition gained through earning a PhD.

Second approach: the visual analysis method

This methodology is identical to the first one, except for one significant difference - the inclusion of a photograph or image of your desired subject. The image should be of a compact size so that it can be placed effortlessly on your nightstand. However, it should also possess ample dimensions to ensure clear visibility from your typical sleeping position, especially when the bedside lamp is illuminated.

Please adhere to the instructions in methodology One, ensuring that after completing the task of transcribing "I can DREAM ABOUT..." etc., you dedicate some time to observe the image. It should be the kind of image that you can vividly recall even when your eyes are closed. After observing the image for a brief period, set it aside, extinguish the light, and proceed to rest, endeavoring to recall the mental representation of the image.

Approach Three: The cognitive visualization technique

This task presents a greater level of difficulty in comparison to the previous two, yet it stands out as the most formidable among them. Follow the same approach that you employed for methodology One. If you desire, you may choose to employ an image in a similar manner as shown in methodology 2. Diminish the intensity of sunlight and reduce the level of noise.

Now visualize the topic of your dream as a moving scene, like a movie or programme, or as an occurrence during which you're collaborating. Please take note: it is essential that the mental image remains a cohesive and uninterrupted sequence, avoiding any fragmentation into disconnected pictures.

Similar to methodology 2, exclusively allow your mental representation to remain within your thoughts: suppress any verbalized cognitions.

Success manifests itself in two ways: primarily, one can observe a correlation between the dreams experienced later in the night and the visualizations that occupied one's thoughts. Furthermore, it will become evident that as you continue to visualize, you will naturally enter a state of slumber, allowing your mind to delve into vivid dreams centered around your desired subject matter.

Step Four: Sammaspati

This method has the capacity to enhance the likelihood of achieving success in envisioning precisely what you intend. Indeed, it is a meditation technique rooted in the Buddhist tradition, and it is highly recommended by esteemed authorities for practitioners of the Western Mystery Tradition, including but not limited to Dion Fortune, Rudolf Steiner, and Aleister Crowley.

Encourage the extension of the nape of the neck and the realignment of the chin. Please allocate a few moments to deliberately unwind, by directing your attention to each individual part of your body in succession and enabling your muscles to relax and release. Breathe naturally. Once you have achieved a state of relaxation, you may then proceed to the subsequent step.

Commence by envisioning your entire day in reverse, commencing from this present moment. For example, if your recent routine involves ascending the stairs, proceeding to the bathroom, and then entering your bedroom, you may envision yourself rising from a seated position and walking in reverse into the bathroom. Subsequently, you would walk in reverse out of the bathroom and descend the steps, facing the opposite direction. It appears as though you have meticulously documented your daily routine and are now viewing it in a distorted manner, akin to a mishandled film reel on a projector or the rapid utilization of the Rewind and Play buttons on a video device.

Additionally, by consciously recollecting the images from the day during your meditation, the likelihood of these images influencing the substance of your dreams is reduced. It will become apparent to you that you will merely unearth sentiments that you experienced during a specific occurrence, of which you may have forgotten, yet they have indelibly impacted your subconscious. Therefore, the remaining subject of your aspirations will be that which you have consciously chosen, without any unintentional thoughts entering your mind.

Step Five: Discernment

The state of lucidity arises from one's discerning response to a situational trigger within a dream, leading to the realization that one is indeed immersed in a dream environment. The aforementioned event is essentially characterized by spontaneity, which may manifest as the observation of one's hands, or any other visual clue, or the occurrence of a situation such as discovering oneself in a state of levitation or flight, among other possibilities. Nevertheless, those events that induce clarity of mind hold no practical value unless one is diligent in developing heightened awareness of the unfolding dream, to an even greater extent than they currently possess. The methodology that has proven to be highly effective in my extensive experience is the cultivation of Discernment.

Discernment pertains to the capacity to ascertain the plausibility of an occurrence within one's dream. For instance, (this occurred in Maine recently), let us consider a scenario in which you envision stepping into an unilluminated space, and instinctively reach for the light switch adjacent to the doorway. The sunlight emerges, subsequently recedes once again. You are making another attempt at the switch and encountering the same result. Now, it is essential that you arc prepared to acknowledge that this is not quite how light switches operate in reality: therefore, you now possess a compelling indication or cue that you are indeed in a dream state.

Strategies For Maintaining Lucidity In Your Dream State

In regards to lucid dreaming, the most challenging aspect invariably lies in the endeavor to remain within these dreams, as it necessitates a certain degree of concentration and attentiveness. The subsequent approaches will facilitate the seamless realization of your aspirations:

Relax

If one desires to prolong their experience within a lucid dream, it is crucial to prioritize relaxation. When an individual becomes excessively excited, they have a tendency to lose awareness of the fact that they were in a state of lucid dreaming and subsequently awaken from their slumber. In order to prolong your stay, it is imperative that you achieve a state of mental clarity and tranquility.

Hand movement

After attaining a state of relaxation, it is imperative to bear in mind the importance of gently rubbing one's hands together, as this practice serves to enhance the duration of one's lucid dreaming experience. This is achieved through the ongoing stimulation of the conscious mind.

Focus

Please make certain that you direct your attention towards your hand during your lucid dream. Ensure to maintain visual contact with them at all times.

Spelling test

Consider the act of mentally spelling a word or engaging in a simple arithmetic calculation during the course of your dream. It is an effective means by which one can actively stimulate the logical faculties of the mind during moments prone to distraction.

Circles

By engaging in circular movements, one can readily transport oneself into a fresh dream setting. The aim is to enhance your level of consciousness.

How to regulate the occurrence of lucid dreaming

If you happen to be among individuals who experience trepidation towards lucid dreaming, there exist various methods of exerting control over this phenomenon. It is possible that this is due to the occurrence of highly distressing dreams. Highlighted below are several actions that must be undertaken in order to mitigate or prevent the occurrence of lucid dreams.

Assume a lateral sleeping position: It is often observed that individuals more frequently experience lucid dreams when they are in a supine posture, as lucid dreaming necessitates a sense of detachment from the physical body, resembling a sensation of levitation or soaring.

Establish a consistent sleep schedule: individuals adept at lucid dreaming generally exhibit tendencies towards light sleep. By diligently adhering to a regular sleep pattern, the likelihood of experiencing lucid dreams can be mitigated.

Engage in television viewing prior to bedtime: By engaging in the act of watching television before retiring for the night, you actively stimulate your mind, inducing a state of fatigue that promotes a deep and restful sleep.

Cease your preoccupation with lucid dreams: by fixating on them, you are more likely to encounter such experiences; therefore, it is best to redirect your attention away from them.

Refrain from consuming caffeine or alcohol prior to bedtime: the consumption of caffeine or alcohol can disrupt your sleep, leading to frequent awakenings and potentially increasing the likelihood of experiencing lucid dreaming.

ERRORS COMMITTED IN THE PROCESS OF LUCID DREAMING

If you are encountering difficulties in consistently achieving lucid dreams, it is likely that errors are being made in the execution of the process. Lucid dreaming is an attainable skill that can be acquired by anyone through the process of learning. In the event of an unsuccessful trial period, there is no need to despair, for it is possible that you are committing some of the errors delineated herein. Consequently, all that is required is a modification in your course of action.

Not adhering to the requisite level of dedication fails to acknowledge that, akin to any acquired proficiency, lucid dreaming demands commitment.

Furthermore, there are individuals who exert excessive effort in their attempts to attain lucid dreaming. However, this approach is likely to hinder the achievement of lucidity.

Experiencing significant limitations in dream recall, a quality that holds considerable significance within the realm of lucid dreaming.

Improper sleep patterns is yet another prevalent error. Adequate sleep plays a crucial role in fostering lucid dreams, as insufficient sleep can hinder the enhancement of dreams by causing discomfort.

By exhibiting impatience, you are committing an error, as the optimal course of action is to maintain composure, adhere to the pertinent methodologies, and permit events to unfold naturally.

Additionally, there are individuals who, upon experiencing their initial lucid dream, become excessively enthusiastic and consequently awaken without attaining a state of complete lucidity.

Failure to properly prepare your mindset will likewise have a detrimental impact on your ability to achieve a lucid dream, as it inhibits the creation of an optimal environment for successful lucid dreaming.

Can The Practice Of Lucid Dreaming Facilitate Personal Transformation?

In contemporary society, nearly all individuals are striving to attain wealth, achieve physical fitness, and attain professional success in their respective vocations. The majority of individuals are actively pursuing their individual objectives. Nevertheless, a vast majority of individuals are devoid of a crucial component, namely, the inherent self-assurance required to attain our objectives. We encounter diverse challenges in the physical realm. Challenges that may impede our progress in realizing our aspirations and goals. However, what if we are able to modify that degree of confidence through our dreams?

In a state of lucid dreaming, we attain the realization that not only are we immersed within the realm of our dreams, but we also possess the discernment that we are the solitary architects of these exceptionally vivid dreamscapes. We possess the capacity to confront the situations that evoke fear in our conscious state while we are in the dream state. Therefore, it facilitates our ability to confront these fears and achieve a sense of inner assurance.

In light of the challenges posed by social anxiety, it has been reported by individuals proficient in lucid dreaming that during their earlier years, they exhibited traits such as shyness, introversion, and aloofness. Establishing interpersonal connections and immersing themselves in social settings elicit feelings of anxiety and apprehension for them. The concept of exerting control over their lucid dreams enabled them to confront these fears. In the majority of their dreams, they encountered multitudes of individuals and delivered orations, performed in vast arenas and amphitheaters. These portrayals facilitated their readiness to confront its tangible manifestations in real life.

Exploring latent fears residing in the depths of one's subconscious - as we engage in lucid dreaming, we navigate the realm of our own subliminal psyche. We might uncover emotions or anxieties that have been deeply ingrained within our subconsciousness for an extended period, unbeknownst to our conscious awareness. The aforementioned fears have the potential to inadvertently detrimentally impact our quality of life. Through the practice of lucid dreaming, we have the capacity to unlock and liberate our fears, ultimately embracing their existence within us.

It facilitates the cultivation of innovative ideas, as creativity is derived from our subconscious realm. When we achieve a state of lucid dreaming, we have the opportunity to harness that exceptional wellspring of creativity. Prominent literary figures, artists, and innovators have adeptly employed these methodologies to their own benefit. Artists were also recognized for deriving inspiration from their dreams. Prominent individuals recognized for their mastery of lucid dreaming are Albert Einstein, Stephen King, Thomas Edison, and James Cameron. Each of them leveraged their ability to attain a state of lucid dreaming in order to facilitate personal transformation and enhance their creative capacities.

Permits the cultivation of novel skillsets - no boundaries or constraints exist within our fantastical realm. We are all capable of honing skills that we have long desired to endeavor. This may encompass activities such as engaging in music, acquiring martial arts skills, creating artistic depictions of landscapes, or crafting speeches that often fall short of excellence in practice. Within the realm of our vivid dreams, we possess the freedom to embody any desired entity. The scope of our abilities is solely determined by the capacity of our minds.

It compels you to reach your utmost potential, as anything is capable of transpiring within the realm of a dream. You might find yourself pursued by a creature, or experiencing apprehension while speaking before an audience, or confronted with your deepest personal anxieties. Lucid dreaming can serve as a valuable tool in conquering one's fears and pushing oneself to the boundaries of their capabilities. Due to your conscious realization of being in a dream, you have been capable of effectively carrying out necessary actions in the face of diverse circumstances or anxieties. Consequently, this training aims to equip you with strategies for managing such situations in your day-to-day experiences.

It is possible to engage in flight - dreams in which one perceives oneself soaring may be construed as emblematic of a sense of liberation or emancipation from constraints imposed either personally or by one's environment. One can experience the capability to accomplish virtually anything. It is indicative of possessing a resolute determination. Engaging in the act of aerial navigation within the realm of your lucid dreaming experience can evoke a sense of authoritative influence over the unfolding events.

Employing lucid dreams as a means of self-transformation has the potential to propel us towards progress, while simultaneously offering a significant cognitive stimulus. By integrating our waking realities with our dream states, we can enhance our capacity to attain favorable transformation. However, prior to reaching this stage, it is imperative to acquire proficiency in lucid dreaming and diligently engage in its practice. That is simply the sole occasion during which that individual can fully leverage this particular skill.

One prominent motivation behind the attraction to becoming adept lucid dreamers stems from the capacity it affords individuals to engage in seemingly unattainable experiences and liberates them within the realm of dreams. After acquiring the ability to induce conscious dreams or lucid dreams, individuals gain the capacity to exercise control over their actions, manipulate the unfolding events, and alter the narrative as per their wishes. This empowers them to engage in further exploration, navigate through time, enhance their running speed, and transcend the bounds of flight, unhindered by any limitations to their potential achievements.

Managing And Addressing Sleep Disorders

Sleeping disorders consistently prove to be a significant impediment to daily life, thereby causing inconvenience during sleep and subsequently impairing overall functionality due to sleep deprivation. This compromises our ability to perform optimally and hinders our effectiveness in fulfilling our responsibilities and obligations. Sleeping disorders hinder cognitive clarity, impair mental acuity, and can induce a persistent burden of stress.

The approach to addressing sleeping disorders varies depending on the specific type of disorder present. Typically, sleep studies are conducted to evaluate the condition, and subsequently, medical professionals may prescribe suitable medications to facilitate deeper sleep for the patient. Furthermore, in certain cases, individuals may receive psychological assistance due to the potential emotional component associated with sleeping disorders. Frequently, sleep disorders are precipitated by the daily pressures of life, which presents a paradoxical situation since these very disorders can also contribute to increased stress levels. This highlights the cyclical nature of the relationship between sleep disorders and stress, necessitating intervention in either one to break the cycle.

The initial method of safeguarding against sleeping disorders and sleep deprivation entails acquiring the knowledge and skills necessary to improve one's sleep. Obtaining improved sleep and experiencing uninterrupted rest for a sufficient duration, without frequent awakenings due to various factors, will typically suffice in alleviating any sleep disorders or stress. There are several methods to enhance one's sleep quality, outlined below.

Ensuring Sufficient Rest – For individuals who experience difficulty falling asleep, it is advisable to retire to bed one hour earlier to allow ample time to unwind. You possess the most intimate knowledge of your own sleep patterns, and it is advisable to allocate a sufficient time frame for sleep when retiring for the night, in order to ensure a minimum of eight hours of recommended sleep. During the morning hours, if you find it challenging to promptly arise from bed at the sound of the alarm, consider configuring the snooze function to activate after a duration of five minutes. This approach enables a gradual awakening and gradual transition into a state of full consciousness, owing to the repetitive nature of the alarm ringing every five minutes.

Refrain from consuming caffeine and sugar in the evening – such as a warm cup of hot chocolate prior to bedtime. That does not facilitate or support your ability to sleep. Chocolate contains sugars and confectionery that provide a subtle energy boost to invigorate the body. Refrain from consuming caffeine starting in the late afternoon. Exercise caution when selecting your consumables, as numerous products, in addition to coffee and tea, may contain caffeine. Soda and certain vitamins are recognized for containing caffeine as well.

Midnight snacking is discouraged, as consuming meals before bed is strongly advised against. Insufficient digestion time within the digestive system leads to an intensified workload, causing one to awaken. Additionally, excessive consumption may lead to acidity, causing discomfort in the gastrointestinal tract and disruption of sleep patterns.

Evening Regimen – this may be more commonly associated with toddlers and young children, don't you agree? Furthermore, this principle is relevant to individuals across all age groups. Establishing a structured evening routine entails adhering to a predetermined schedule aimed at promoting a tranquil and subdued atmosphere leading up to bedtime.

Ensure optimal sleeping conditions by regulating the temperature to your preference. Neither excessively hot nor excessively cold. In the event of a warm evening, it is advised to allow for proper ventilation by keeping the window ajar and arranging for the use of a lightweight blanket or alternatively, activating the air conditioning system. During the winter season, it is advised to stack a generous number of high-quality, comfortable duvets for optimal warmth and comfort.

An optimal environment that ensures the room temperature is neither excessively warm nor excessively cold, as these conditions can exacerbate the severity of a nocturnal terror. Please ensure that you or a child has an ample supply of blankets and slightly ajar the door to allow some light to permeate the space. Steer clear of excessively bulky or restrictive winter sleepwear; compensate by adding extra layers of blankets.

Acquire a State of Comfort – particularly when dealing with children, it is crucial to ensure their comfort prior to bedtime. Facilitating their engagement in their preferred game or television program, followed by reciting their beloved book and performing their favored melody, instigates constructive thinking and contributes to the alleviation of nocturnal disturbances.

Do not engage in a Count Down - a prevalent issue experienced by individuals in the workforce who find it challenging to commence their workday due to inadequate sleep, thereby exerting unnecessary mental strain on themselves at night by engaging in a count down. This is the act of reclining in bed and engaging in a conscious inner dialogue, wherein one mentally reminds oneself that by succumbing to slumber at that moment, one shall be afforded the luxury of a continuous eight-hour period of restful sleep. Subsequently, they experience restlessness and agitation upon contemplating the potential loss of valuable sleeping time. They find themselves pondering over the dwindling minutes allotted for slumber, only to become increasingly anxious as the thought surfaces, "I still have seven hours to sleep," followed by, "Why am I still awake when I have five hours remaining?" Employing a countdown approach induces stress immediately prior to sleep and presents no beneficial effects.

If an individual experiences a sleeping disorder, it is advisable to be vigilant and actively seek feedback from one's partner regarding potential manifestations such as snoring, restlessness, vocalization, excessive movement, or any other atypical behavior observed while in bed. Identify a potential sleeping disorder at an early stage and take proactive measures to address it before it intensifies.

www.ingramcontent.com/pod-product-compliance
Lightning Source LLC
Chambersburg PA
CBHW050250120526
44590CB00016B/2292